I0759521

A Cosy Chocolate Cookbook

First published in Great Britain in
2026 by Hamlyn, an imprint of
Octopus Publishing Group Ltd
Carmelite House
50 Victoria Embankment
London EC4Y 0DZ
www.octopusbooks.co.uk

An Hachette UK Company
www.hachette.co.uk

The authorized representative in the EEA
is Hachette Ireland, 8 Castlecourt Centre,
Dublin 15, D15 XTP3, Ireland
(email: info@hbgi.ie)

Distributed in the US by
Hachette Book Group
1290 Avenue of the Americas,
4th and 5th Floors,
New York, NY 10104

Distributed in Canada by
Canadian Manda Group,
664 Annette St.,
Toronto, Ontario,
Canada M6S 2C8

ISBN 978-0-6006-3985-5
eISBN 978-0-6006-3989-3

A CIP catalogue record for this book is available from the British Library.

Printed and bound in China.

10 9 8 7 6 5 4 3 2 1

Publisher: Lucy Pessell
Designers: Isobel Platt & Kath Anderson
Editor: Tim Leng
Assistant Editor: Samina Rahman
Production Controller:
Lucy Carter & Nic Jones

Picture Acknowledgements:
iStock: 5second 43, AnaMOMarques 38, apomares 50, bhofack2 71, Chatri Attanatwong 11, fcafotodigital 8, IvanSpasic 41, Metkalova 20, nerudol 4, 66; Octopus Publishing Group: 25, 33, 35, 53, 55, 63, 65, 13, 23, 69.

This FSC® label means that materials used for the product have been responsibly sourced.

A Cosy Chocolate Cookbook

Recipes for irresistible brownies, bakes, cupcakes and more

Eloise Goode

hamlyn

CONTENTS

Chocolate is one of those foods that's almost universally loved – some may even go so far as to consider it an essential treat! It's safe to say that there's no other food as tantalizing: it's moreish and gratifying, can make us feel nostalgic for the bars we enjoyed as children and comfort us when we're sad. It gives us energy, satisfies our sweet tooth and relieves our hunger. Whether you like your chocolate to be milk, white or dark, in a bar, cup or cake, one thing is certain: we can't get enough of this enticing sweet treat.

Within these pages you'll discover a collection choc-full of delectable delights, from cakes and bakes to cookies and whoopies – all with chocolate at their very heart. A little chocolate treat is the answer to many of life's questions, so why not indulge your cocoa cravings with these irresistibly sweet recipes – they're easy to make and even better to devour!

So, grab your favourite chocolate and prepare your bowls, tins and trays! It's time to roll up your sleeves and begin with a Chilli Hot Chocolate – let's choc and roll! Enjoy the sweeter side of life, one delicious recipe at a time.

CHILLI HOT CHOCOLATE

Cook time 10 minutes

175 g (6 oz) plain dark chocolate, broken into pieces
1 large pinch of chilli powder
2 tablespoons caster (superfine) sugar
2 large pinches of ground cinnamon
2 vanilla pods, split lengthways
600 ml (1 pint) milk

To serve
200 ml (7 fl oz) whipping cream, whipped
grated plain dark chocolate

Place the chocolate, chilli powder, sugar, cinnamon, vanilla pods and milk into a pan and heat gently until the chocolate has melted.

Bring to the boil and whisk until the chocolate is very smooth and frothy.

Remove the vanilla pods.

Pour the hot chocolate into 4 warmed mugs and top with the whipped cream and grated chocolate, and serve immediately.

CLASSIC
TREATS

CHOCOLATE CHIP COOKIES

MAKES 16

Prep time 10 minutes
Cook time 15 minutes

125 g (4 oz) unsalted butter, softened
175 g (6 oz) soft light brown sugar
1 teaspoon vanilla extract
1 egg, lightly beaten
1 tablespoon milk
200 g (7 oz) plain (all-purpose) flour
1 teaspoon baking powder
250 g (8 oz) plain dark chocolate chips

Beat together the butter and sugar in a large bowl until pale and fluffy. Mix in the vanilla extract, then gradually beat in the egg. Stir in the milk. Sift in the flour and baking powder, then fold in. Stir in the chocolate chips.

Drop level tablespoonfuls of the mixture, about 3.5 cm (1½ inches) apart, onto a large baking sheet lined with baking parchment, then lightly press with a floured fork. Bake in a preheated oven, 180°C (350°F), Gas Mark 4, for 15 minutes, or until lightly golden. Transfer to a wire rack to cool.

DOUBLE CHOCOLATE COOKIES

MAKES 18

Prep time 15 minutes, plus chilling & cooling
Cook time 10 minutes

150 g (5 oz) butter
150 g (5 oz) golden caster (superfine) sugar
1 egg yolk
250 g (8 oz) self-raising flour, plus extra for dusting
25 g (1 oz) cocoa powder
100 g (3½ oz) plain dark, milk or white chocolate, broken into squares

Cream the butter and sugar together until pale and fluffy. Add the egg yolk, then sift in the flour and cocoa powder. Mix together until a firm dough is formed. Knead lightly on a floured surface, then wrap and chill for 20 minutes to firm up.

Roll out the dough on a sheet of nonstick baking paper and cut out 18 circles, using a 5 cm (2 inch) cutter. Put squares of chocolate on top of each circle of dough. Transfer the paper and biscuits to a baking sheet.

Bake in a preheated oven, 190°C (375°F), Gas Mark 5, for 10 minutes. Cool for 10 minutes, before transferring to a wire rack.

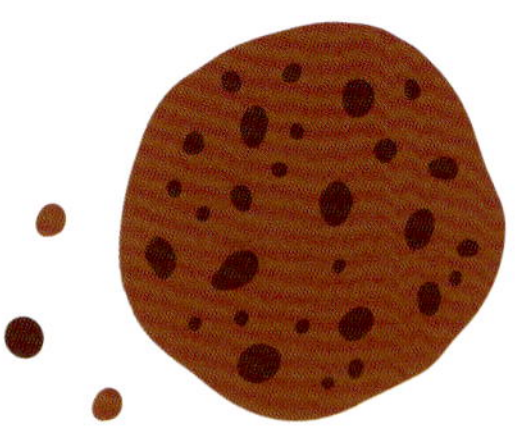

CHOCOLATE CORNFLAKE BARS

CUTS INTO 12 BARS

Prep time 10 minutes, plus chilling
Cook time 3 minutes

200 g (7 oz) milk chocolate, broken into pieces
2 tablespoons golden syrup
50 g (2 oz) olive oil spread
125 g (4 oz) cornflakes

Melt the chocolate with the golden syrup and olive oil spread in a bowl over a pan of simmering water.

Stir in the cornflakes and mix well together.

Grease a 28 x 18 cm (11 x 7 inch) tin. Turn the mixture into the tin, press down using the back of a spoon, and chill until set. Cut into 12 bars.

CHOCOLATE FUDGE BROWNIES

SERVES 8

Prep time 10 minutes
Cook time 30 minutes

200 g (7 oz) butter
200 g (7 oz) dark chocolate, chopped
175 g (6 oz) soft dark brown sugar
150 g (5 oz) caster (superfine) sugar
4 eggs
50 g (2 oz) ground almonds
75 g (3 oz) plain (all-purpose) flour
vanilla ice cream, to serve

Gently melt the butter and chocolate together in a 23 cm (9 inch) ovenproof frying pan. Remove from the heat and cool for a couple of minutes.

Beat together the sugars and eggs, then stir in the chocolate mixture followed by the almonds and flour.

Wipe the rim of the frying pan with a damp piece of kitchen paper or cloth to neaten, then pour the mixture into the pan. Bake in a preheated oven, 180°C (350°F), Gas Mark 4, for 25 minutes until just set. Serve warm with vanilla ice cream.

CLASSIC CHOCOLATE BROWNIES

SERVES 8–10

Prep time 10 minutes
Cook time 30 minutes

125 g (4 oz) reduced-fat sunflower spread
2 eggs
125 g (4 oz) light soft brown sugar
75 g (3 oz) self-raising flour
50 g (2 oz) cocoa powder, sieved, plus extra to decorate
50 g (2 oz) plain dark chocolate, chopped
1 teaspoon chocolate extract
salt

Grease and line an 18 cm (7 inch) square deep cake tin.

Beat together the sunflower spread, eggs and sugar. Stir in the flour and cocoa powder, then add the chocolate and chocolate extract. Stir in 1 teaspoon boiling water and a pinch of salt.

Transfer the mixture to the prepared tin and bake in a preheated oven, 190°C (375°F), Gas Mark 5, for 30 minutes, or until a skewer inserted into the centre comes out clean. Leave to cool in the tin, then cut into squares. Dust with a little cocoa powder to serve.

RICH CHOCOLATE MOUSSE

SERVES 4

Prep time 5 minutes, plus chilling
Cook time 3–4 minutes

175 g (6 oz) plain dark chocolate, broken into pieces
100 ml (3 fl oz) double (heavy) cream
3 eggs, separated
cocoa powder, for dusting

Put the chocolate and cream in a heatproof bowl set over a saucepan of gently simmering water (do not let the bowl touch the water) and stir until the chocolate has melted. Leave to cool for 5 minutes, then beat in the egg yolks one at a time.

Whisk the egg whites in a separate clean bowl until stiff, then lightly fold into the chocolate mixture until combined. Spoon the mousse into 4 dessert glasses or cups and chill in the refrigerator for at least 2 hours. Dust with cocoa powder before serving.

BAKED CHOCOLATE CHEESECAKE

SERVES 2

Prep time 10 minutes, plus cooling
Cook time 45 minutes

25 g (1 oz) unsalted butter, melted
75 g (3 oz) ratafia or ameretti biscuits, crushed
150 g (5 oz) cream cheese
25 g (1 oz) caster (superfine) sugar
50 g (2 oz) mascarpone cheese
50 g (2 oz) dark plain chocolate, melted
1 egg
1 egg yolk

To decorate
crème fraîche
chocolate shavings

Melt the butter in a saucepan. Add the crushed biscuits and mix well. Divide the mixture between two 10 cm (4 inch) tart tins, and press down to form the cheesecake bases.

Place the cream cheese, sugar, mascarpone and chocolate in a small pan and warm over a gentle heat, stirring until the mixture is melted and blended.

Remove from the heat, allow to cool and then beat in the egg and the yolk.

Divide the chocolate mixture between the tart tins and place them on a baking sheet. Bake in a in a preheated oven, 180°C (350°F), Gas Mark 4, for 45 minutes, or until set. Remove from the oven and leave the cheesecakes to cool before transferring them to the refrigerator. Chill until required, then decorate with a dollop of crème fraîche and chocolate shavings.

WHITE CHOCOLATE TORTE

SERVES 8

Prep time 10 minutes, plus cooling
Cook time 45 minutes

475 g (15 oz) white chocolate
125 g (4 oz) butter, plus extra for greasing
3 large eggs, separated
125 g (4 oz) golden caster (superfine) sugar
75 g (3 oz) wholemeal (whole wheat) self-raising flour, sifted
50 g (2 oz) ground almonds

Melt 225 g (7½ oz) of the chocolate with the butter in a bowl over a pan of simmering water. Reserve the rest of the chocolate for decoration.

Beat the egg yolks and sugar until pale, thick and foamy. Slowly whisk in the melted chocolate,then fold the flour and ground almonds into the mixture.

Whisk the egg whites in a large clean bowl until softly peaking. Beat a large spoonful of the egg whites into the chocolate mixture to loosen it slightly, then fold in the remainder using a large metal spoon.

Grease a 20 cm (8 inch) springform tin and line with a greaseproof cake liner or nonstick baking paper. Pour the mixture into the tin and bake in a preheated oven, 180°C (350°F), Gas Mark 4, for 45 minutes, or until a skewer inserted into the centre comes out clean.

Cool in the tin for 10 minutes, then release and remove the sides of the tin and continue cooling. Grate half the reserved white chocolate and melt the rest in a bowl over a pan of simmering water. Spread the melted chocolate over the top of the cooled cake, then scatter over the gratings.

CHOCOLATE DEVIL'S FOOD CAKE

SERVES 12

Prep time 30 minutes, plus cooling
Cook time 35 minutes

225 g (7½ oz) plain (all-purpose) flour
1 teaspoon bicarbonate of soda
50 g (2 oz) cocoa powder
125 g (4 oz) butter
250 g (8 oz) light muscovado sugar
3 eggs
250 ml (8 fl oz) milk
1 tablespoon lemon juice

For the frosting
175 g (6 oz) plain dark chocolate
75 g (3 oz) milk chocolate
3 tablespoons golden caster (superfine) sugar
300 ml (½ pint) soured cream

In a large bowl, sift together the flour, bicarbonate of soda and cocoa powder. In a separate bowl, cream together the butter and half the sugar until soft and fluffy. Gradually whisk in the eggs, then whisk in the rest of the sugar. Mix the milk with the lemon juice to sour it, then fold into the flour mixture until smoothly combined.

Grease two 20 cm (8 inch) cake tins and line the bases with nonstick baking paper. Spoon the mixture equally into the prepared tins and level over the surface of both.

Bake in a preheated oven, 180°C (350°F), Gas Mark 4, for 30 minutes until risen, springy to the touch and shrinking away from the edges of the tin. Cool in the tins for 10 minutes, then upturn the cakes onto a wire rack to cool.

To make the frosting, melt the dark and milk chocolate together in a bowl over a pan of simmering water, then remove from the heat and whisk in the sugar and soured cream to make the frosting.

Slice each cake in half horizontally to make 4 layers. Put one layer on a serving dish and spread with one-quarter of the frosting. Top with another cake layer, then some more frosting. Continue layering cake and frosting, ending with a layer of frosting on top.

SWEET &
STICKY
TREATS

CHOCOLATE & APRICOT CRUNCH

CUTS INTO 16 SQUARES

Prep time 10 minutes, plus chilling & freezing

200 g (7 oz) orange-flavoured plain dark chocolate (70% cocoa solids)
125 g (4 oz) unsalted butter
1 tablespoon golden syrup
4 meringue nests, broken into small pieces
125 g (4 oz) chocolate chip cookies, broken into pieces
150 g (5 oz) ready-to-eat dried apricots, chopped
cocoa powder, for dusting

Line an 18 x 28 cm (7 x 11 inch) cake tin with nonstick baking paper. Place the chocolate, butter and golden syrup in a small saucepan and heat gently, stirring occasionally, until smooth and shiny.

Place all remaining ingredients in a large bowl and mix well, then pour over the chocolate mixture. Stir until all the ingredients are evenly coated.

Tip the mixture into the prepared tin and level the mixture with the back of a spoon. Place in the freezer for 10 minutes, then chill in the refrigerator for a further 10 minutes until firm.

Run a knife around the edge of the tin, turn out on to a board and remove the baking paper. Dust the surface with cocoa powder and cut into 16 slices. Store any leftover bars in an airtight container for up to 3–4 days.

WICKED CHOCOLATE PUDDING

SERVES 6

Prep time 20 minutes
Cook time 2 hours

75 g (3 oz) butter
150 g (5 oz) light muscovado sugar
finely grated rind of 1 orange
2 eggs
150 g (5 oz) self-raising flour
25 g (1 oz) cocoa powder
½ teaspoon bicarbonate of soda
100 g (3½ oz) milk chocolate, chopped
pouring cream or ready-made custard, to serve

For the sauce
125 g (4 oz) light muscovado sugar
75 g (3 oz) butter
4 tablespoons orange juice
50 g (2 oz) dates, stoned and chopped

Put the butter, sugar, orange rind and eggs in a large bowl, then sift in the flour, cocoa powder and bicarbonate of soda and beat well until creamy. Stir in the chocolate.

Grease the inside of a 1.2 litre (2 pint) pudding basin and line the base with nonstick baking paper. Tip the mixture into the basin and level the surface. Cover with a double thickness of nonstick baking paper and a sheet of foil, securing them under the rim of the basin with string.

Pour 5 cm (2 inches) of water into a saucepan large enough to hold the basin and bring to the boil. Lower in the basin into the pan, reduce the heat to a simmer, and cover the pan with a lid. Steam for 1¾ hours, topping up the water occasionally, if necessary.

To make the sauce, heat the sugar, butter and orange juice gently in a small saucepan until the sugar dissolves. Bring to the boil and boil for 1 minute. Stir in the dates and cook for 1 minute. To serve, invert the pudding onto a serving plate and pour the sauce over the top. Serve with pouring cream or custard.

CHOCOLATE & CARDAMOM POTS

SERVES 4

Prep time 10 minutes
Cook time 8 minutes

200 g (7 oz) good-quality dark chocolate, broken into squares
seeds from 8–10 cardamom pods, crushed
2 tablespoons coffee liqueur
2 tablespoons extra virgin olive oil
3 large eggs, separated
4 tablespoons whipped double (heavy) cream
sifted cocoa powder, for dusting

Place the chocolate in a small, heatproof bowl with the cardamom, coffee liqueur and olive oil and set over a pan of barely simmering water. Leave the chocolate to melt very slowly without stirring for about 8 minutes.

Remove the bowl from the heat and quickly beat in the egg yolks. Set aside while you put the egg whites in a large bowl and whisk until stiff. Stir 1 tablespoon of the beaten whites into the chocolate mixture to slacken it, then carefully fold in the remaining egg whites with a metal spoon.

Divide the mixture between 4 ramekins or pretty coffee cups. Cover and chill for 2 hours, or until required. Serve with a little whipped cream and a dusting of cocoa powder.

AMARETTI & CHOCOLATE CUSTARD

SERVES 4

Prep time 20 minutes, plus chilling
Cook time 55–65 minutes

175 g (6 oz) granulated sugar
125 ml (4 fl oz) cold water
2 tablespoons cocoa powder
4 tablespoons boiling water
2 eggs
2 egg yolks
65 g (2½ oz) amaretti biscuits, finely crushed
450 ml (¾ pint) milk
150 ml (¼ pint) strong black coffee
chocolate curls or a few amaretti biscuits, crumbled, to decorate

In a small saucepan, dissolve 125 g (4 oz) of the sugar in the measured cold water, stirring occasionally, then increase the heat and boil for 5 minutes without stirring until golden brown, keeping a watchful eye towards the end of the cooking time.

Mix the cocoa powder with 2 tablespoons of the boiling water in a bowl. Mix the remaining sugar with the eggs, egg yolks and biscuits in a separate bowl.

Take the syrup off the heat as soon as it caramelizes. Add the remaining boiling water and tilt to mix. Pour into a 900 ml (1½ pint) ovenproof dish. Tilt to coat the base and halfway up the sides. Stand in a roasting tin.

Pour the milk into the drained caramel pan and bring just to the boil. Stir the cocoa mix into the egg mixture, then gradually whisk in the hot milk, followed by the coffee. Slowly pour into the caramel-lined dish.

Fill the roasting tin with hot water halfway up the sides of the dish. Cook in a preheated oven, 160°C (325°F), Gas Mark 3, for 50–60 minutes until the custard has just set but still wobbles slightly in the centre.

Take dish out of tin, leave to cool, then chill for 4–5 hours or overnight. To turn out, stand in just-boiled water for 10 seconds, then invert on a plate. Decorate with chocolate or biscuits.

COFFEE CHOCOLATE BAVAROIS

SERVES 10

Prep time 45 minutes, plus freezing & chilling
Cook time 10 minutes

- **1 litre (1¾ pints) single (light) cream**
- **150 g (5 oz) plain dark chocolate, chopped**
- **2 teaspoons cornflour (cornstarch)**
- **150 g (5 oz) golden caster (superfine) sugar**
- **8 egg yolks**
- **25 g (1 oz) powdered gelatine**
- **1 tablespoon espresso coffee, fresh, very strong**
- **4 tablespoons coffee liqueur**

Line a 1 kg (2 lb) loaf tin with nonstick baking paper and place in the freezer to chill.

Heat half the cream gently in a pan. Add the chocolate and stir until melted. Remove from the heat.

Put half the cornflour, half the sugar and 4 egg yolks in a bowl. Put the remaining cornflour, sugar and yolks in a second bowl. Stir, then slowly whisk the chocolate cream into one bowl. Transfer to the pan and heat gently, stirring until slightly thickened and smooth. Whisk in half the powdered gelatine, then pour into a jug.

Pour half the chocolate cream into the prepared loaf tin. Freeze uncovered, on a flat surface, for 45 minutes until just set.

Combine the remaining cream, espresso coffee and coffee liqueur in a pan over a low heat. Whisk this into the mixture in the second bowl, transfer to the pan and warm through. Add the rest of the gelatine and whisk together. Remove from the heat and pour into a jug.

Pour half the coffee cream over the set chocolate cream and refreeze for another 30 minutes, or until just set. Pour over the remaining chocolate cream and freeze for 20 minutes until just set, then pour on the final coffee cream layer. Chill for 4 hours. Run a knife around the sides, turn onto a board and slice to serve.

CARAMEL CHOCOLATE FONDANTS

SERVES 6

Prep time 10 minutes
Cook time 20 minutes

200 g (7 oz) unsalted butter, plus extra for greasing
225 g (7½ oz) plain dark chocolate, broken into small pieces
50 g (2 oz) plain (all-purpose) flour, plus extra for dusting
3 large eggs, plus 2 large egg yolks
75 g (3 oz) soft light brown sugar
6 dessertspoons dulce de leche or thick caramel sauce
ice cream, to serve

Place the butter and chocolate in a small saucepan over a low heat and warm until just melted. Stir gently, then set aside.

Meanwhile, grease 6 x 200 ml (7 fl oz) freezer-proof and heatproof ramekins or metal pudding moulds with butter and dust lightly with flour, then place on a baking sheet.

Place the eggs plus egg yolks and sugar in a large bowl and beat with a hand-held electric whisk until thick and creamy. Fold in the flour and melted chocolate.

Spoon the mixture into the prepared dishes and dollop 1 spoonful of the dulce de leche or caramel sauce into the centre of each one, then cover with a little of the chocolate mixture. Place in the freezer for 8–10 minutes.

Remove from the freezer and bake in a preheated oven, 200°C (400°F), Gas Mark 6, for 12–14 minutes until almost firm but still with a slight wobble in the centre. Leave to cool in the dishes for 2 minutes, then invert onto serving dishes and serve each with a scoop of ice cream.

CHOCOLATE & PISTACHIO SOUFFLÉS

SERVES 6

Prep time 10 minutes
Cook time 30 minutes

butter, for greasing
25 g (1 oz) pistachio nuts, ground
150 g (5 oz) plain dark chocolate (72% cocoa solids), broken into small pieces
4 eggs, separated
100 g (3½ oz) caster (superfine) sugar
2 teaspoons cornflour (cornstarch)
cocoa powder or icing (confectioners') sugar, for dusting (optional)

Grease 6 x 175 ml (6 fl oz) ramekins, then lightly dust with 1 tablespoon of the ground pistachios to cover the base and sides. (This will help the soufflés to rise.) Place on a baking sheet.

Melt the chocolate in a heatproof bowl set over a saucepan of gently simmering water, then leave to cool slightly.

Meanwhile, whisk the egg whites in a clean large bowl with a hand-held electric whisk until stiff, then gradually whisk in half the sugar until the mixture is thick and glossy.

Stir the remaining sugar, egg yolks and cornflour into the cooled chocolate mixture. Gently fold some of the egg white mixture into the chocolate mixture, then gently fold in the remainder, with the remaining pistachios. Spoon into the prepared ramekins and spread the tops level, then clean the edges.

Place in a preheated oven, 190°C (375°F), Gas Mark 5, for 20 minutes, or until risen. Dust with cocoa powder or icing sugar (if using) and serve immediately.

CHOCOLATE & BANANA MELT

SERVES 4

Prep time 5 minutes
Cook time 2–4 minutes

8 slices of white bread, crusts removed
75 g (3 oz) dark chocolate, finely chopped
1 large banana, sliced
50 g (2 oz) marshmallows, chopped
1 tablespoon of vegetable oil, for frying
vanilla ice cream, to serve (optional)

Place half the bread slices on the work surface and top each with the chocolate, banana and marshmallows. Top with the remaining bread slices and gently press down.

Heat the oil in a large frying pan over a medium heat and add the sandwiches to the pan. Cook for 1–2 minutes, then flip over gently and cook for a further 1–2 minutes until golden. Serve immediately with vanilla ice cream, if desired.

PEACH & CHOCOLATE VACHERIN

SERVES 6–8

Prep time 30 minutes, plus cooling
Cook time 1½–1¾ hours

4 egg whites
125 g (4 oz) caster (superfine) sugar
100 g (3½ oz) light muscovado sugar
150 g (5 oz) plain dark chocolate, broken into pieces

For the filling
150 ml (¼ pint) double (heavy) cream
150 g (5 oz) Greek yogurt
2 tablespoons caster (superfine) sugar
3 ripe peaches, pitted and sliced

Line 2 baking sheets with nonstick baking paper and draw an 18 cm (7 inch) circle on each.

Whisk the egg whites in a large bowl until stiff, moist-looking peaks form. Mix the sugars together, then whisk in the sugar, 1 tablespoonful at a time, and continue whisking for 1–2 minutes until very thick and glossy.

Divide the mixture between the lined baking sheets and spread into circles of even thickness within the marked lines. Bake in a preheated oven, 110°C (225°F), Gas Mark ¼, for 1½–1¾ hours, or until the meringues may be easily lifted off the paper. Leave to cool in the switched-off oven.

Melt the chocolate, then spread over the underside of each meringue, leaving about one-third of the chocolate in the bowl for decoration. Leave the meringues to harden, chocolate-side up.

When ready to serve, make the filling. Whip the cream until it forms soft swirls, then fold in the yogurt and sugar. Put one of the meringue circles on a serving plate, chocolate-side up, and spread with the cream, then arrange peach slices on top. Cover with the second meringue, chocolate-side down. Decorate the top with the remaining melted chocolate, drizzled over randomly.

WHITE CHOCOLATE & STRAWBERRY CHEESECAKE

SERVES 6–8

Prep time 10 minutes, plus chilling
Cook time 10 minutes

150 g (5 oz) digestive biscuits, crushed
75 g (3 oz) unsalted butter, melted
200 g (7 oz) white chocolate, broken into small pieces
500 g (1 lb) mascarpone cheese
25 g (1 oz) icing (confectioners') sugar, sifted
200 g (7 oz) strawberries, hulled and sliced
white chocolate curls, to decorate

Stir the biscuits into the melted butter and press into the base of a 20 cm (8 inch) loose-bottomed round cake tin. Chill while you make the filling.

Melt the chocolate in a heatproof bowl set over a saucepan of gently simmering water, stirring occasionally.

Place the mascarpone in a bowl and whisk in the icing sugar until smooth. Whisk in the chocolate, then spread the mixture over the cheesecake base.

Chill for 15 minutes, then arrange the strawberries over the top and decorate with the chocolate curls. Serve immediately or chill until ready to serve.

CANDIED ORANGE & CHOCOLATE TART

SERVES 8

Prep time 35 minutes, plus chilling & cooling
Cook time 1¼ hours

200 g (7 oz) caster (superfine) sugar
4 tablespoons water
2 medium oranges, thinly sliced
flour, for dusting
470 g (15 oz) shop-bought all-butter sweet shortcrust pastry
100 g (3½ oz) butter, at room temperature, plus extra for greasing
100 g (3½ oz) ground almonds
2 eggs, beaten
100 g (3½ oz) plain dark chocolate, melted

Add half the sugar and the water to a saucepan and heat gently until the sugar has dissolved. Add the orange slices and cook over a low heat for 30 minutes until the oranges are tender, the peel is soft and almost translucent and most of the syrup has evaporated. Set aside to cool.

Roll the pastry out thinly on a lightly floured surface to fit a greased 24 cm (9½ inch) fluted loose-bottomed tart tin. Press the pastry over the base and sides of the tin. Trim off the excess with scissors so that it stands a little above the top of the tin. Chill for 15 minutes.

Bake the tart blind for 10 minutes. Remove the paper and baking beans and bake for a further 5 minutes. Remove from the oven and reduce the oven temperature to 180°C (350°F), Gas Mark 4.

Cream the butter and the remaining sugar in a bowl until light and fluffy. Add the ground almonds, gradually beat in the eggs until smooth, then set aside.

Reserve 10 of the best orange slices to decorate, then drain and chop the rest. Stir the melted chocolate into the almond mixture, followed by the chopped oranges. Spread into the tart case. Arrange the reserved orange slices in a ring on top and bake for 30 minutes. Leave to cool for 30 minutes, then remove from the tin.

CHOCOLATE CREAM PIE

SERVES 6–8

Prep time 45 minutes, plus chilling & cooling
Cook time 55 minutes–1 hour

235 g (7 ½ oz) plain (all-purpose) flour
15 g (½ oz) cocoa powder
pinch of salt
125 g (4 oz) butter, diced
2½–3 tablespoons cold water
flour, for dusting

For the filling

150 g (5 oz) plain dark chocolate, broken into pieces
500 g (1lb) cream cheese, softened
100 g (3½ oz) caster (superfine) sugar
1 tablespoon plain (all-purpose) flour
1 teaspoon vanilla extract
3 eggs

Add the flour, cocoa powder, salt and butter to a large mixing bowl. Rub together with your fingertips until the mixture resembles fine crumbs. Gradually mix in just enough water to enable the crumbs to be squeezed together to form a soft but not sticky dough. Knead very lightly until smooth.

Roll the dough out on a lightly floured surface a little larger than a greased 23 cm (9 inch) fluted loose-bottomed tart tin 3.5 cm (1½ inches) deep. Press the pastry over the base and sides and trim off the excess so it stands just above the top of the tin. Prick the base with a fork, then chill for 15 minutes. Blind bake the tart for 15 minutes. Remove the paper and baking beans and bake for a further 5 minutes. Remove from the oven and reduce the oven temperature to 150°C (300°F), Gas Mark 2.

To make the filling, melt the chocolate in a bowl over a pan of hot water. The put the cream cheese in a bowl, add the sugar, flour and vanilla extract, then gradually beat in the eggs until smooth. Ladle about one-third into the chocolate bowl and mix until smooth.

Pour the cheese mixture into the tart case, then pipe the chocolate mixture over the top and swirl together with the handle of a teaspoon for a marbled effect. Bake for 30–35 minutes until set around the edges, beginning to crack and the centre still wobbles slightly. Leave to cool in the turned-off oven. When cool, refrigerate overnight. Remove the pie from the tin, place on a plate and slice to serve.

CHOCOLATE FILIGREE TORTE

SERVES 10

Prep time 30 minutes, plus cooling & chilling
Cook time 20–25 minutes

3 eggs
75 g (3 oz) caster (superfine) sugar
50 g (2 oz) plain (all-purpose) flour
25 g (1 oz) cocoa powder

For the filling
2 teaspoons powdered gelatine
3 tablespoons cold water
200 g (7 oz) plain dark chocolate
500 g (1 lb) mascarpone cheese, at room temperature
75 g (3 oz) caster (superfine) sugar
1 teaspoon vanilla extract
200 g (7 oz) Greek yogurt
4 tablespoons hot water

Whisk the eggs and sugar in a bowl over a pan of hot water until thickened. Remove from the heat and whisk for 2 minutes. Sift over the flour and cocoa powder, then fold in.

Grease and line a 23 cm (9 inch) springform or loose-based cake tin, and pour in the mixture. Bake in a preheated oven, 190°C (375°F), Gas Mark 5, for 15 minutes until just firm. Cool on a wire rack.

To make the filling, sprinkle the gelatine over the cold water in a bowl and leave for 5 minutes. Cut the cake in half and put the bottom half back in the cake tin. Stand the bowl of gelatine in a pan of hot water until the gelatine has melted.

Melt 175 g (6 oz) of the chocolate over a pan of simmering water. Beat the mascarpone in a bowl with the sugar, vanilla extract, yogurt and hot water. Whisking well, gradually pour the melted gelatine into the mascarpone mixture. Spoon half into a separate bowl and beat in the chocolate. Pour the chocolate mix into the tin. Cover with the top sponge, then the remaining mascarpone (if this has started to set, beat in a little hot water). Level the surface and chill for several hours.

Lift the cake out of the tin, removing the nonstick baking paper and transfer to a serving plate. Melt the remaining chocolate and drizzle it over the top. Chill until ready to serve.

CUPCAKES
& MUFFINS

CHOCOLATE ORANGE CUPCAKES

MAKES 12

Prep time 20 minutes, plus cooling
Cook time 25 minutes

125 g (4 oz) lightly salted butter, softened
125 g (4 oz) caster (superfine) sugar
2 eggs
125 g (4 oz) self-raising flour
25 g (1 oz) cocoa powder
½ teaspoon baking powder
finely grated rind of 1 orange
candied orange peel shavings, to decorate (optional)

For the icing
100 g (3½ oz) plain chocolate, chopped
100 g (3½ oz) unsalted butter, softened
125 g (4 oz) icing (confectioners') sugar
2 tablespoons cocoa powder

Line a 12-hole cupcake tray with paper cases. Put the butter, sugar, eggs, flour, cocoa powder, baking powder and orange rind in a bowl and beat with a hand-held electric whisk for about 1 minute until light and creamy. Divide the mixture evenly between the cases.

Bake in a preheated oven, 180°C (350°F), Gas Mark 4, for 20 minutes, or until risen and just firm to the touch. Cool on a wire rack.

To make the icing, melt the chocolate and leave to cool. Beat together the butter, icing sugar and cocoa powder in a bowl until smooth and creamy. Stir in the melted chocolate. Pipe or swirl the icing over the tops of the cakes and decorate with candied orange peel shavings, if desired.

TRIPLE CHOCOLATE CUPCAKES

MAKES 12

Prep time 30 minutes, plus cooling & setting
Cook time 40 minutes

150 g (5 oz) butter or margarine
150 g (5 oz) caster (superfine) sugar
175 g (6 oz) self-raising flour
3 eggs
1 teaspoon vanilla extract

To decorate

100 g (3½ oz) white chocolate, chopped
100 g (3½ oz) milk chocolate, chopped
100 g (3½ oz) plain chocolate, chopped
40 g (1½ oz) unsalted butter

Whisk the butter or margarine, sugar, flour, eggs and vanilla extract in a mixing bowl until light and creamy.

Line a 12-hole cupcake tray with paper cases. Divide the mixture evenly between the cases and bake in a preheated oven, 180°C (350°F), Gas Mark 4, for 18–20 minutes until risen and just firm to the touch. Transfer to a wire rack to cool.

Meanwhile, put the white, milk and plain chocolate in separate microwave-proof or heatproof bowls and add one-third of the butter to each. Melt all the chocolate, either one at a time in a microwave or by setting each bowl over a saucepan of very gently simmering water, stirring occasionally until smooth.

Spread the melted white chocolate over 4 of the cakes using a small palette knife.

Put 2 tablespoons of the melted milk and plain chocolate in separate piping bags, fitted with writing nozzles. Spread the milk chocolate over 4 more of the cakes and pipe lines of plain chocolate over the milk chocolate.

Spread the plain chocolate over the remaining 4 cakes and scribble with lines of piped white chocolate. Leave to set.

MOCHA CUPCAKES

MAKES 12

Prep time 15 minutes, plus cooling
Cook time 20 minutes

250 ml (8 fl oz) water
250 g (8 oz) caster (superfine) sugar
125 g (4 oz) unsalted butter
2 tablespoons cocoa powder, sifted
½ teaspoon bicarbonate of soda
2 tablespoons instant coffee
225 g (7½ oz) self-raising flour
2 eggs, lightly beaten
12 chocolate-coated coffee beans, to decorate (optional)

For the drizzle
150 g (5 oz) plain dark chocolate, broken into pieces
150 g (5 oz) unsalted butter, diced
2 tablespoons golden syrup

Line a 12-hole cupcake tray with paper cases. Put the water and sugar in a saucepan and heat gently, stirring, until the sugar has dissolved. Stir in the butter, cocoa powder, bicarbonate of soda and instant coffee and bring to the boil. Simmer for 5 minutes, remove from the heat and set aside to cool.

Beat the flour and eggs into the cooled coffee and chocolate mixture until smooth. Divide the mixture evenly between the cases. Bake in a preheated oven, 180°C (350°F), Gas Mark 4, for 20 minutes until risen and firm. Transfer to a wire rack to cool.

To make the drizzle, put the chocolate, butter and golden syrup in a heatproof bowl set over a saucepan of gently simmering water, stirring until melted. Remove from the heat and leave to cool to room temperature. Drizzle over the cupcakes, top with a chocolate coffee bean, if desired, and leave to set.

CHOCOLATE PEANUT CUPCAKES

MAKES 12

Prep time 25 minutes, plus cooling & setting
Cook time 30 minutes

150 g (5 oz) lightly salted butter, softened
250 g (8 oz) caster (superfine) sugar
3 eggs
150 g (5 oz) self-raising flour
25 g (1 oz) cocoa powder
½ teaspoon baking powder
50 g (2 oz) salted peanuts
3 tablespoons water
75 ml (3 fl oz) double (heavy) cream
25 g (1 oz) unsalted butter
100 g (3½ oz) plain chocolate, chopped
1 tablespoon golden syrup

Line a 12-hole cupcake tray with paper cases. Put the lightly salted butter, 150 g (5 oz) of the sugar, the eggs, flour, cocoa powder and baking powder in a bowl and beat with a hand-held electric whisk for about 1 minute until light and creamy. Divide the mixture evenly between the cases.

Bake in a preheated oven, 180°C (350°F), Gas Mark 4, for 20 minutes, or until risen and just firm to the touch. Cool on a wire rack.

Chop the peanuts finely. Put the remaining sugar in a small saucepan with the measured water and heat gently until the sugar has dissolved. Bring to the boil and boil rapidly for 4–5 minutes until the syrup has turned a pale golden colour. Dip the base of the pan in cold water to prevent further cooking.

Add 50 ml (2 fl oz) of the cream and the unsalted butter to the syrup and heat very gently, stirring, to make a smooth caramel. Stir in the chopped nuts and leave until cool but not set. Spoon over the cupcakes.

Melt the chocolate with the remaining cream and golden syrup in a small saucepan over a gentle heat. Spoon over the cakes and leave to set.

BANOFFEE CHOCOLATE MUFFINS

MAKES 6

Prep time 10 minutes, plus cooling
Cook time 22 minutes

225 g (7½ oz) self-raising flour, sifted
2 tablespoons cocoa powder, sifted
100 g (3½ oz) caster (superfine) sugar
100 g (3½ oz) dark chocolate chips
2 eggs
2 small ripe bananas, mashed
50 ml (2 fl oz) vegetable oil
125 g (4 oz) natural yogurt
warmed toffee sauce, to serve

Line a 12-hole cupcake tray with paper cases. In a bowl, mix the flour, cocoa powder, sugar and 75 g (3 oz) of the chocolate chips together.

Combine the eggs, bananas, oil and yogurt in a bowl, then pour the wet ingredients into the dry and mix to barely combine. Divide the mixture evenly between the cases and scatter over the remaining chocolate chips.

Bake in the preheated oven, 180°C (350°F), Gas Mark 4, for 18–22 minutes until risen and firm to the touch. Cool slightly on a wire rack and serve warm, drizzled with warm toffee sauce.

CHILLI CHOCOLATE CHIP MUFFINS

MAKES 8

Prep time 20 minutes
Cook time 20 minutes

200 g (7 oz) self-raising flour
50 g (2 oz) cocoa powder
1 teaspoon baking powder
150 g (5 oz) soft light brown sugar
1 egg
250 ml (8 fl oz) milk
50 g (2 oz) butter, melted
125 g (4 oz) chilli chocolate, chopped, or plain dark chocolate, chopped, and a pinch of chilli powder
75 g (3 oz) pecan nuts, toasted and roughly ground
spray olive oil, for oiling

Cut a 15 cm (6 inch) square from baking parchment and use it as a template to cut 7 more. Open out flat and set aside.

Sift the flour, cocoa powder and baking powder into a bowl and stir in the sugar. Beat together the egg, milk and melted butter in a jug. Add to the dry ingredients and stir together using a large metal spoon until just combined. Fold in the chocolate or chocolate and chilli powder and pecan nuts.

Spray each square of baking parchment with oil and press each piece into the hole of a muffin tray. Spoon the mixture into the lined holes and bake in a preheated oven, 200°C (400°F), Gas Mark 6, for 20 minutes until risen and golden. Transfer to a wire rack to cool slightly, then serve warm.

WHITE CHOCOLATE & VANILLA MUFFINS

MAKES 12

Prep time 15 minutes, plus cooling
Cook time 25 minutes

125 g (4 oz) plain (all-purpose) flour
200 g (7 oz) self-raising flour
½ teaspoon baking powder
125 g (4 oz) white chocolate, coarsely grated or chopped
½ teaspoon bicarbonate of soda
200 g (7 oz) golden caster (superfine) sugar
rind of 1 lemon, finely grated
200 g (7 oz) butter, melted
3 large eggs
125 ml (4 fl oz) soured cream
1 teaspoon vanilla extract
125 ml (4 fl oz) sweet dessert wine
icing (confectioners') sugar, for dusting

Sift both flours and the baking powder into a large bowl. Add the chocolate, bicarbonate of soda, sugar and lemon rind and mix everything together.

Mix together the melted butter, eggs, soured cream and vanilla extract in a large jug. Pour the wet ingredients into the dry ingredients and stir together to combine.

Line a 12-hole muffin tin with paper cases. Spoon the mixture into the cases and bake in a preheated oven, 180°C (350°F), Gas Mark 4, for 25 minutes until risen, firm, pale golden and a cocktail stick comes out clean when it is inserted into the centre of a muffin.

Transfer to a wire rack to cool. Pierce the muffins several times with a cocktail stick and pour over the sweet wine. Dust with icing sugar to serve.

PEANUT BUTTER & CHOCOLATE MINI MUFFINS

MAKES 12

Prep time 10 minutes
Cook time 20 minutes

25 g (1 oz) unsalted butter
100 g (3½ oz) crunchy peanut butter
150 g (5 oz) plain (all-purpose) flour
1½ teaspoons baking powder
pinch of salt
75 g (3 oz) soft light brown sugar
1 large egg
125 ml (4 fl oz) buttermilk
50 g (2 oz) milk chocolate chunks or chips

Line a 12-hole mini muffin tin with paper cases. Place the butter and peanut butter in a small saucepan over a low heat and warm until just melted. Stir gently, then set aside.

Meanwhile, sift the flour, baking powder and salt into a large bowl, then stir in the sugar. Whisk together the egg, buttermilk and melted butters in a jug. Pour into the dry ingredients and stir until just combined.

Spoon the mixture into the cases, then scatter over the chocolate chunks or chips.

Bake in a preheated oven, 200°C (400°F), Gas Mark 6, for 10–15 minutes until risen and golden. Serve warm.

CHOCOLATE RASPBERRY FRIANDS

MAKES 10

Prep time 20 minutes
Cook time 20 minutes

100 g (3½ oz) lightly salted butter
75 g (3 oz) plain chocolate, at room temperature
100 g (3½ oz) ground almonds
125 g (4 oz) golden caster (superfine) sugar
40 g (1½ oz) plain (all-purpose) flour
3 egg whites
150 g (5 oz) fresh raspberries
icing (confectioners') sugar, for dusting (optional)

Line 10 holes of a 12-hole cupcake tray with paper cases. Melt the butter in a small saucepan and leave to cool. Coarsely grate the chocolate – if the chocolate is brittle and difficult to grate, try softening it in a microwave for a few seconds first, but take care not to overheat and melt it.

Mix together the ground almonds, 75 g (3 oz) of the caster sugar and the flour in a large bowl. Stir in the melted butter and grated chocolate until just combined.

Whisk the egg whites in a thoroughly clean bowl until peaking. Gradually whisk in the remaining caster sugar. Using a large metal spoon, fold half the egg whites into the chocolate mixture to lighten it, then fold in the remainder until evenly combined.

Divide the mixture evenly between the cases and scatter the raspberries on top.

Bake in a preheated oven, 200°C (400°F), Gas Mark 6, for 15 minutes, or until golden and just firm to the touch. Transfer to a wire rack to cool. Serve dusted with icing sugar.

LITTLE
TREATS

DOUBLE CHOCOLATE TRUFFLES

MAKES 24

Prep time 45 minutes, plus chilling
Cook time 8 minutes

250 ml (8 fl oz) double (heavy) cream
200 g (7 oz) plain dark chocolate, chopped
3–4 tablespoons brandy or rum
2 tablespoons cocoa powder, sifted
200 g (7 oz) plain dark chocolate
crystallized violets

Pour the cream into a small pan and bring to the boil. Take the pan off the heat and add the chopped chocolate. Leave to stand until it has melted, then stir in the brandy or rum and mix until smooth. Chill for 4 hours until the truffle mixture is firm.

Line a baking sheet with nonstick baking paper and dust with the cocoa powder. Scoop a little truffle mixture onto a teaspoon, then transfer it to a second spoon and back to the first again, making a well-rounded egg shape (or use a melon baller). Slide the truffle onto the cocoa-dusted paper. Repeat until all the mixture is used up. Chill again for 2 hours, or overnight if possible, until firm.

Melt the remaining chocolate in a bowl over a pan of simmering water. Stir well, then, holding 1 truffle at a time on a fork over the bowl, spoon melted chocolate over the top to coat it. Place the truffles on a piece of nonstick baking paper on a tray. Swirl a little chocolate over the top of each with a spoon and finish with a crystallized violet.

Chill for at least 1 hour, then pack into petit-four cases.

RICH CHOCOLATE MACARONS

MAKES 12

Prep time 20 minutes, plus standing & cooling
Cook time 20 minutes

50 g (2 oz) icing (confectioners') sugar
50 g (2 oz) ground almonds
4 tablespoons cocoa powder
2 egg whites
100 g (3 ½ oz) caster (superfine) sugar

For the filling

5 tablespoons double (heavy) cream
100 g (3 ½ oz) plain dark chocolate, chopped

Line 2 baking sheets with nonstick baking paper. Put the icing sugar, ground almonds and cocoa powder in a food processor and blend to a very fine consistency.

Put the egg whites in a thoroughly clean bowl and whisk until peaking. Gradually whisk in the sugar, a tablespoonful at a time and whisking well after each addition, until thick and very glossy. Add the almond mixture to the bowl and use a metal spoon to stir the ingredients together to combine.

Place the egg mixture in a piping bag fitted with a 1 cm (½ inch) plain nozzle, and pipe 24 x 3 cm (1¼ inch) rounds onto the baking sheets. Tap the baking sheet firmly to smooth the surfaces of the macarons slightly, then leave to stand for 30 minutes. Bake in a preheated oven, 160°C (325°F), Gas Mark 3, for about 15 minutes, or until the surfaces feel crisp. Leave to cool before carefully peeling away the paper.

To make the filling, heat the cream in a small saucepan until bubbling up around the edges but not boiling. Remove from the heat and stir in the chocolate. Leave the chocolate to melt, stirring frequently, until smooth. Once the chocolate is cool and thickened enough to hold its shape, use to sandwich the macarons together in pairs. Keep in a cool place until ready to serve.

CHOCOLATE VIENNESE WHIRLS

MAKES ABOUT 15

Prep time 10 minutes, plus cooling
Cook time 8–10 minutes

200 g (7 oz) unsalted butter, softened
50 g (2 oz) icing (confectioners') sugar, sifted
125 g (4 oz) self-raising flour
2 tablespoons cocoa powder
4 tablespoons cornflour (cornstarch)
1–3 teaspoons milk

Line 2 baking sheets with nonstick baking paper. Place the butter and icing sugar in a bowl and beat together using a hand-held electric whisk until light and fluffy. Sift in the flour, cocoa powder and cornflour and mix to a smooth paste, adding just enough of the milk to form a piping consistency.

Spoon the mixture into a piping bag fitted with a star-shaped nozzle, then pipe about 15 whirls onto the prepared baking sheets.

Bake in a preheated oven, 200°C (400°F), Gas Mark 6, for 8–10 minutes until firm. Leave to cool on the sheets for 1 minute, then transfer to wire racks to cool completely.

WALNUT & WHITE CHOCOLATE COOKIES

MAKES ABOUT 25

Prep time 15 minutes, plus cooling
Cook time 12–15 minutes

1 egg
150 g (5 oz) soft light brown sugar
2 tablespoons caster (superfine) sugar
1 teaspoon vanilla extract
125 ml (4 fl oz) vegetable oil, plus extra for greasing
65 g (2½ oz) plain (all-purpose) flour
3 tablespoons self-raising flour
¼ teaspoon ground cinnamon
25 g (1 oz) shredded coconut
175 g (6 oz) walnuts, toasted and chopped
125 g (4 oz) white chocolate chips

Grease 2 baking sheets and line with nonstick baking paper. In a bowl, beat the egg and sugars together until light and creamy. Stir in the vanilla extract and oil. Sift in the flours and cinnamon, then add the coconut, walnuts and chocolate and mix well.

Form rounded tablespoonfuls of the mixture into balls and place on the prepared baking sheets, pressing the mixture together with your fingertips if it is crumbly.

Bake in a preheated oven, 180°C (350°F), Gas Mark 4, for 12–15 minutes, or until golden. Leave to cool slightly on the sheets, then transfer to a wire rack to cool completely.

CHOCOLATE BISCUIT BITES

CUTS INTO 8 SLICES

Prep time 15 minutes, plus cooling & chilling

300 g (10 oz) plain chocolate, broken into pieces
2 tablespoons milk
125 g (4 oz) butter, melted, plus extra for greasing
125 g (4 oz) digestive biscuits, lightly crushed
2 packets white chocolate buttons
2 packets milk chocolate buttons

Grease an 18 cm (7 inch) cake tin or similar. Put the chocolate and milk in a bowl set over a pan of simmering water, making sure the bowl does not touch the water, and leave until the chocolate has melted, stirring occasionally. Stir in the butter. Remove the bowl from the heat and leave until cool, but not solid.

Mix the biscuit pieces with the white and milk chocolate buttons, then stir the mixture into the melted chocolate, then pour it into the tin and push it down gently. Refrigerate for at least 3 hours until firm, then cut into slices and serve.

CHOCOLATE BLONDIE BITES

MAKES ABOUT 36

Prep time 15 minutes
Cook time 30 minutes

40 g (1½ oz) lightly salted butter, plus extra for greasing
200 g (7 oz) white chocolate
2 eggs
65 g (2½ oz) caster (superfine) sugar
1 teaspoon vanilla bean paste
75 g (3 oz) self-raising flour, sifted
50 g (2 oz) blanched almonds, roughly chopped

Grease and line a 20 cm (8 inch) square cake tin with nonstick baking paper.

Chop half the chocolate into small pieces and set aside. Roughly chop the remainder and put in a heatproof bowl with the butter. Rest the bowl over a saucepan of gently simmering water and leave until melted.

Beat together the eggs, sugar and vanilla bean paste in a separate bowl. Beat in the melted chocolate mixture. Add the flour, almonds and chopped chocolate and stir well. Turn into the tin and spread into the corners.

Bake in a preheated oven, 190°C (375°F), Gas Mark 5, for 25 minutes, or until golden and the centre feels just firm to the touch. Leave to cool completely, then remove from the tin and cut into small squares.

MINI CHOCOLATE LOGS

MAKES 6

Prep time 20 minutes
Cook time 10 minutes

3 eggs
125 g (4 oz) golden caster (superfine) sugar, plus 2 tablespoons for sprinkling
100 g (3½ oz) plain (all-purpose) flour
25 g (1 oz) cocoa powder
1 tablespoon hot water
butter, for greasing
6 tablespoons shop-bought chocolate spread

Whisk the eggs with the sugar for 10 minutes until thick. Sift over the flour and cocoa powder and gently fold in, along with the measured hot water.

Grease a 33 x 23 cm (13 x 9 inch) Swiss roll tin and line with nonstick baking paper. Pour the mixture into the tin and bake in a preheated oven, 220°C (425°F), Gas Mark 7, for 10 minutes until risen and just firm.

Sprinkle a large sheet of nonstick baking paper with sugar. Upturn the cake onto the baking paper and carefully peel off the lining. Use a sharp knife to trim off all the crisp edges.

Cut the cake in half to make 2 long strips, then cut each strip into 3 pieces. As you cut the cake, cut the nonstick baking paper underneath as well and use a ruler to make sure all the strips are an equal width. Spread each piece of cake with 1 tablespoon of chocolate spread. Roll up each cake and remove the baking paper before serving.

CHOCOLATE ORANGE MADELEINES

MAKES 12

Prep time 15 minutes, plus cooling
Cook time 15 minutes

75 g (3 oz) butter, melted and cooled, plus extra for greasing
75 g (3 oz) self-raising flour, plus extra for dusting
2 large eggs
1 teaspoon orange extract
1 teaspoon finely grated orange rind
75 g (3 oz) caster (superfine) sugar
pinch of salt
100 g (3½ oz) plain dark or milk chocolate, broken into small pieces

Lightly brush a 12-hole madeleine tray, friand tray or mini muffin tin with melted butter and dust lightly with flour.

Place the eggs, orange extract, orange rind, sugar and salt in a large bowl and beat with a hand-held electric hand whisk until pale and thick and the whisk leaves a trail when lifted above the mixture. Sift in the flour, then add the melted butter and fold gently until combined.

Spoon the mixture into the prepared tray and bake in a preheated oven, 200°C (400°F), Gas Mark 6, for 8–10 minutes until risen and golden.

Meanwhile, melt the chocolate in a heatproof bowl set over a saucepan of gently simmering water, ensuring the bowl does not touch the water. Stir gently and set aside.

Remove the madeleines from the oven and transfer to a wire rack. Once cool to the touch, spread some melted chocolate over each cake. Leave to set in a cool place for a

CHOCOLATE ICED FANCIES

MAKES 16

Prep time 45 minutes, plus cooling
Cook time 25 minutes

100 g (3½ oz) lightly salted butter, softened, plus extra for greasing
125 g (4 oz) plain dark chocolate, chopped
125 g (4 oz) light muscovado sugar
2 eggs
50 g (2 oz) self-raising flour
25 g (1 oz) cocoa powder
50 g (2 oz) ground almonds
5 tablespoons ship-bought chocolate hazelnut spread

For the icing
200 g (7 oz) plain dark chocolate, chopped
2 tablespoons golden syrup
15 g (½ oz) lightly salted butter
50 g (2 oz) milk chocolate, chopped

Grease and line a 15 cm (6 inch) square tin with nonstick baking paper. Grease the paper.

Melt the chocolate in a heatproof bowl set over a saucepan of gently simmering water, ensuring the bowl does not touch the water. Stir gently and set aside. Beat together the butter and sugar in a bowl until pale and creamy. Gradually beat in the eggs, adding a little flour to prevent the mixture curdling. Stir in the melted chocolate.

Sift the flour and cocoa powder over the bowl. Add the ground almonds and stir in gently. Pour into the tin and level the surface. Bake in a preheated oven, 160°C (325°F), Gas Mark 3, for about 20 minutes until risen and just firm to the touch. Transfer to a wire rack to cool.

Cut the cake into 16 squares and, using a palette knife, spread a little mound of chocolate hazelnut spread on the top of each one.

To make the icing, melt the plain dark chocolate with the golden syrup and butter until smooth and glossy. Separately melt the milk chocolate. Spoon a little of the plain chocolate mixture over each cake and spread around the sides with a palette knife. Using a teaspoon, drizzle lines of milk chocolate over each cake.

CHOCOLATE PEANUT BUTTER WHOOPIE PIES

MAKES 15

Prep time 20 minutes, plus cooling
Cook time 20 minutes

300 g (10 oz) self-raising flour
2 teaspoons baking soda
50 g (2 oz) cocoa powder
175 g (6 oz) light brown sugar
1 egg, beaten
75 ml (3 fl oz) vegetable oil
150 ml (¼ pint) buttermilk
75 ml (3 fl oz) boiling water
125 g (4 oz) cream cheese
100 g (3½ oz) smooth peanut butter
200 g (7 oz) icing (confectioners') sugar
100 g (3½ oz) plain dark chocolate

Line a large baking sheet with nonstick baking paper. Place the flour, baking soda, cocoa power and light brown sugar in a large bowl. Mix the egg, oil and buttermilk with the boiling water and stir into the dry ingredients until well mixed.

Spoon about 30 tablespoonfuls onto the prepared sheet, making sure they are spaced well apart. Bake in a preheated oven, 180°C (350°F), Gas Mark 4, for 10–12 minutes, or until just firm. Leave to cool.

Beat together the cream cheese and peanut butter until smooth. Sift in the icing sugar and beat until well combined. Pipe or spoon the icing over 15 halves, then sandwich the remaining 15 on top.

Melt the chocolate in a small bowl set over a pan of simmering water, making sure the water does not touch the bottom of the bowl. Drizzle over the whoopie pies before serving.

FROSTED CHOCOLATE WHOOPIES

MAKES 12–14

Prep time 20 minutes, plus cooling
Cook time 15 minutes

butter, for greasing
150 g (5 oz) self-raising flour
¼ teaspoon bicarbonate of soda
25 g (1 oz) cocoa powder
100 g (3 ½ oz) golden caster (superfine) sugar
2 tablespoons vanilla sugar
1 egg
3 tablespoons vegetable oil
1 tablespoon milk
50 g (2 oz) plain or milk chocolate, chopped

For the filling

100 g (3½ oz) cream cheese
2 tablespoons icing (confectioners') sugar, sifted
1 teaspoon finely grated orange rind
few drops of orange extract (optional)

Grease a large baking sheet.

Put the flour, bicarbonate of soda, cocoa powder and sugars in a bowl. Beat the egg with the vegetable oil and milk and add to the dry ingredients. Beat together to form a thick paste, adding a little more milk if the mixture feels crumbly.

Using floured hands, roll the mixture into 24–28 cherry-sized balls. Space well apart on the baking sheet and flatten slightly.

Bake in a preheated oven, 200°C (400°F), Gas Mark 6, for 12 minutes until the mixture has spread and is pale golden. Transfer to a wire rack to cool.

To make the frosting, beat together the cream cheese, icing sugar, orange rind and extract (if using). Use to sandwich the cakes together. Melt the chocolate and spread over the tops of the whoopies.

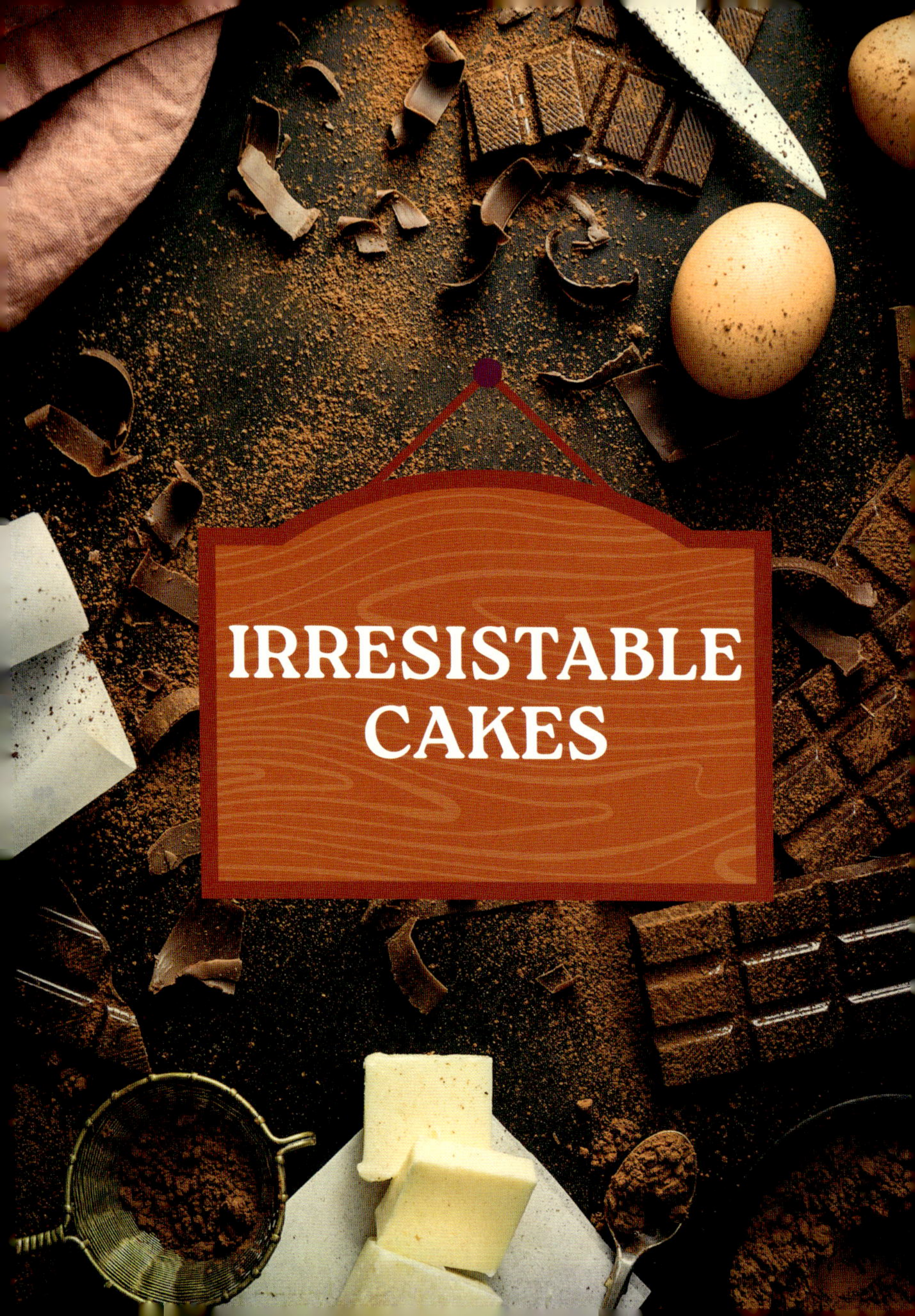
IRRESISTABLE
CAKES

FLOURLESS CHOCOLATE CAKE

SERVES 12

Prep time 25 minutes
Cook time 1 hour

125 g (4 oz) blanched almonds, roughly chopped
125 g (4 oz) Brazil nuts, roughly chopped
225 g (7½ oz) plain dark chocolate, chopped into 5 mm (¼ inch) pieces
225 g (7½ oz) slightly salted butter, softened, plus extra for greasing
4 eggs, separated
225 g (7½ oz) golden caster (superfine) sugar
cocoa powder, for dusting

To serve
fresh raspberries
vanilla ice cream

Put the almonds, Brazil nuts and chocolate in a food processor and process to the consistency of ground almonds. Beat together the butter, egg yolks and 175 g (6 oz) of the sugar in a bowl until pale and creamy. Stir in the chocolate mixture.

Whisk the egg whites in a large clean bowl with a hand-held electric whisk until peaking. Gradually whisk in the remaining sugar, a spoonful at a time. Stir a quarter of the mixture into the creamed mixture using a large metal spoon. Add the remaining egg whites and fold in gently to mix.

Spoon the mixture into a greased and lined 23 cm (9 inch) loose-bottomed or springform cake tin and level the surface. Bake in a preheated oven, 160°C (325°F), Gas Mark 3, for about 1 hour, or until just firm to the touch and a skewer inserted into the centre comes out clean.

Leave to cool in the tin (the centre of the cake will sink slightly), then remove the ring and base and dust with cocoa powder. Serve with raspberries and vanilla ice cream.

CHOCOLATE TRUFFLE CAKE

SERVES 8

Prep time 15 minutes
Cook time 40 minutes

250 g (8 oz) plain dark chocolate, broken into pieces
125 g (4 oz) unsalted butter
50 ml (2 fl oz) double (heavy) cream
4 eggs, separated
125 g (4 oz) caster (superfine) sugar
2 tablespoons cocoa powder, sifted, plus extra for dusting
icing (confectioners') sugar, for dusting

To serve
whipped cream
strawberries

Melt the chocolate, butter and cream together in a heatproof bowl set over a saucepan of gently simmering water. Remove from the heat and leave to cool for 5 minutes.

Whisk the egg yolks with 75 g (3 oz) of the sugar until pale and stir in the cooled chocolate mixture.

Whisk the egg whites in a large clean bowl until softly peaking, then whisk in the remaining sugar. Fold into the egg yolk mixture with the sifted cocoa powder until evenly incorporated.

Pour the cake mixture into a greased and base-lined 23 cm (9 inch) springform cake tin that has been lightly dusted all over with a little extra cocoa powder. Bake in a preheated oven, 180°C (350°F), Gas Mark 4, for 35 minutes.

Leave to cool in the tin for 10 minutes, then turn out onto a serving plate. Serve in wedges, while still warm, with whipped cream and strawberries.

CHOCOLATE & BEETROOT FUDGE CAKE

SERVES 12

Prep time 20 minutes, plus cooling & chilling
Cook time 45–50 minutes

250 g (8 oz) plain (all-purpose) flour
75 g (3 oz) cocoa powder
1 teaspoon bicarbonate of soda
300 g (10½ oz) light muscovado sugar
250 g (8 oz) cooked fresh beetroot, chopped
300 ml (½ pint) almond milk
100 ml (3½ fl oz) sunflower oil, plus extra for oiling
2 teaspoons vanilla extract
1 tablespoon cider vinegar

For the icing
150 g (5 oz) vegan spread
225 g (8 oz) icing (confectioners') sugar
1 teaspoon vanilla extract
150 g (5 oz) dairy-free plain dark chocolate, melted and cooled

Sift the flour, cocoa powder and bicarbonate of soda together into a large bowl. Stir in the sugar and set aside.

Blend the beetroot in a blender or food processor until smooth. With the motor running, pour in the almond milk, oil, vanilla extract and vinegar.

Tip the blended beetroot into the dry ingredients and stir until thoroughly mixed. Pour the mixture into an oiled and base-lined 20 cm (8 inch) springform cake tin and bake in a preheated oven, 180°C (350°F), Gas Mark 4, for 45–50 minutes until just firm to the touch. Leave to cool in the tin.

Meanwhile, make the icing. Beat the spread, icing sugar and vanilla extract together in an electric mixer until soft, then gradually beat in the melted chocolate until well combined and smooth. Refrigerate for 1 hour. Release the cooled cake from the tin and spread with the chilled icing.

CHOCOLATE & HAZELNUT GÂTEAU

SERVES 8–10

Prep time 30 minutes, plus chilling
Cook time 1–1¼ hours

5 eggs, separated
300 g (10 oz) caster (superfine) sugar
1 tablespoon cornflour (cornstarch)
125 g (4 oz) blanched hazelnuts, toasted and finely ground
cocoa powder, for dusting

For the filling

250 g (8 oz) plain dark chocolate, broken into pieces
200 ml (7 fl oz) double (heavy) cream

For the chocolate hazelnuts

50 g (2 oz) hazelnuts
50 g (2 oz) plain dark chocolate, melted

Whisk the egg whites in a large clean bowl until stiff. Whisk in the sugar, a tablespoonful at time, until it has all been added. Whisk again until the meringue mixture is thick and glossy. Fold in the cornflour and hazelnuts, then spoon the mixture into a large piping bag fitted with a 1 cm (½ inch) plain nozzle.

Draw a 23 cm (9 inch) circle on 3 sheets of nonstick baking paper. Starting in the centre of each circle, pipe the mixture in a continuous coil, finishing just within the outer line. Bake all 3 in a preheated oven, 150°C (300°F), Gas Mark 2, for 1–1¼ hours until lightly golden and dried out. Remove from the oven and transfer to a wire rack to cool completely.

To make the filling, heat the chocolate and cream in a heatproof bowl set over a saucepan of simmering water, stirring occasionally until the chocolate has melted. Remove from the heat and leave to cool, then chill in the refrigerator for 1 hour until thickened.

Make the chocolate hazelnuts. Using a fork, dip the hazelnuts into the melted chocolate until coated. Leave to set on baking paper.

Beat the filling until light and fluffy and use it to sandwich the 3 meringue layers together. Decorate with the chocolate hazelnuts and serve dusted with cocoa powder.

CHOCOLATE BOMBE CAKE

SERVES 20

Prep time 1 hour, plus cooling
Cook time 1¼ hours

250 g (8 oz) butter
250 g (8 oz) golden caster (superfine) sugar
few drops vanilla extract
5 eggs, lightly beaten
250 g (8 oz) self-raising flour, plus extra for dusting
100 g (3½ oz) white chocolate chips
100 g (3½ oz) plain dark chocolate chips
25 g (1 oz) cocoa powder
75 g (3 oz) warm apricot jam

For the syrup
50 g (2 oz) golden caster (superfine) sugar
100 ml (3½ fl oz) water
50 ml (2 fl oz) orange liqueur

For the marzipan
1 tablespoon orange liqueur
50 g (2 oz) cocoa powder
450 g (14½ oz) white marzipan

Cream together the butter, sugar and vanilla extract until pale and fluffy, then gradually beat in the eggs. Fold in the flour. Spoon half the mixture into a separate bowl. Add the white chocolate chips to 1 bowl and the plain dark chocolate chips and cocoa powder to the other. Mix each until combined.

Grease a 23 cm (9 inch) dome-shaped tin or heatproof bowl and dust with flour. Spoon in the mixtures alternately, then run a knife through it to create the marble effect. Bake in a preheated oven, 180°C (350°F), Gas Mark 4, for 1–1¼ hours. Leave in the tin for 15 minutes, then turn out onto a wire rack and cool for a further 30 minutes.

To make the syrup, boil the sugar and water in a pan until the liquid becomes syrupy. Remove from the heat, and add the liqueur.

For the marzipan, knead the liqueur and cocoa powder into the marzipan. Roll out two-thirds between 2 sheets of nonstick baking paper to a 40 cm (16 inch) circle, then mould large ripples across it by using your fingertips to gently pinch and pull sections of the marzipan upwards.

Turn the cake onto a serving plate. Spoon over the syrup and brush with apricot jam. Drape the marzipan over and trim off the excess at the base. Pat the sides to make an edge.

Roll out the remaining marzipan and cut 20 x 2.5 cm (1 inch) flower shapes. Arrange the small flowers at the base of the cake.

TOFFEE & CHOCOLATE CAKE

SERVES 10

Prep time 20 minutes
Cook time 45 minutes

175 g (6 oz) plain (all-purpose) flour
25 g (1 oz) cocoa powder
½ teaspoon bicarbonate of soda
½ teaspoon baking powder
200 g (7 oz) light muscovado sugar
1 egg
4 tablespoons milk
1 teaspoon vanilla extract
65 g (2½ oz) slightly salted butter, diced, plus extra for greasing
100 g (3½ oz) plain dark chocolate, chopped
125 ml (4 fl oz) water
chocolate curls, to decorate

For the topping

40 g (1½ oz) very soft unsalted butter
200 g (7 oz) ready-made caramel or toffee sauce

Mix together the flour, cocoa powder, bicarbonate of soda, baking powder and sugar in a bowl. Beat together the egg, milk and vanilla extract in a small bowl.

Put the butter, chocolate and water in a saucepan and heat very gently, stirring frequently, until melted and smooth. Add the egg mixture, melted butter and chocolate mixture to the dry ingredients and stir well to mix.

Spoon the mixture into a greased and lined 23 cm (9 inch) round or 20 cm (8 inch) square cake tin and level the surface. Bake in a preheated oven, 180°C (350°F), Gas Mark 4, for 30–40 minutes until just firm to the touch and a skewer inserted into the centre comes out clean. Loosen the edges, turn out onto a wire rack and peel off the lining paper. Leave to cool.

To make the topping, beat together the butter and caramel or toffee sauce in a bowl. Transfer the cake to a serving plate, spread the topping over the top of the cake and scatter with chocolate curls.

COCONUT & CHOCOLATE CAKES

MAKES 8

Prep time 20 minutes, plus cooling
Cook time 30 minutes

- **75 g (3 oz) sweetened shredded coconut**
- **175 g (6 oz) self-raising flour**
- **1 teaspoon baking powder**
- **175 g (6 oz) golden caster (superfine) sugar**
- **3 large eggs, lightly beaten**
- **175 g (6 oz) butter, melted, plus extra for greasing**
- **200 g (7 oz) milk chocolate**

Reserve one-third of the coconut and put the rest in a large bowl. Add the flour, baking powder, sugar, eggs and melted butter. Mix together well until smooth.

Grease and line the base of 8 heart-shaped moulds, approximately 5 cm (2 inch) in diameter. Spoon the mixture into the moulds and bake in a preheated oven, 180°C (350°F), Gas Mark 4, for 20 minutes until the cakes are risen and a skewer inserted into the centre comes out clean. Turn out onto a wire rack to cool, placing the rack over a baking sheet.

Melt the chocolate in a bowl over a pan of simmering water. Use a palette knife to spread the chocolate around the sides of the cakes, then pour the rest of the chocolate over the top of the cakes, allowing it to trickle down the sides.

Sprinkle over the reserved coconut to decorate and allow to set before serving.

CHOCOLATE RIPPLE LOAFCAKE

SERVES 10

Prep time 15 minutes, plus cooling
Cook time 1½ hours

200 g (7 oz) plain dark chocolate
200 g (7 oz) butter, plus extra for greasing
1 teaspoon ground mixed spice
175 g (6 oz) golden caster (superfine) sugar
3 eggs
2 teaspoons vanilla extract
225 g (7½ oz) self-raising flour
½ teaspoon baking powder
100 g (3½ oz) plain dark chocolate, chopped

Melt the chocolate in a bowl over a pan of simmering water and stir in 25 g (1 oz) of the butter and the mixed spice.

Place the remaining butter, sugar, eggs and vanilla extract in a bowl. Sift the flour and baking powder into the bowl and beat until light and fluffy.

Grease the base and long sides of a 1 kg (2 lb) loaf tin. Spoon one-quarter of the mixture into the tin. Spread one-third of the chocolate mixture over the cake mixture. Repeat the layering of the cake mixture and chocolate sauce, finishing with a layer of cake mixture. Sprinkle with the chopped chocolate.

Bake in a preheated oven, 180°C (350°F), Gas Mark 4, for 1¼ hours, or until risen and a skewer inserted into the centre comes out clean. Leave in the tin for 10 minutes, then transfer to a wire rack to cool.

BANANA & CHOCOLATE RING

SERVES 12

Prep time 20 minutes, plus cooling
Cook time 1 hour

200 g (7 oz) plain dark chocolate
175 g (6 oz) butter, plus extra for greasing
250 g (8 oz) self-raising flour, sifted
1 teaspoon baking powder
150 g (5 oz) light muscovado sugar
rind of 1 lemon, finely grated
3 eggs
150 g (5 oz) white chocolate, broken into pieces
3 small bananas, mashed
200 g (5 oz) white chocolate, broken into pieces
125 g (4 oz) white chocolate chips

Melt the plain dark chocolate with 25 g (1 oz) of butter in a bowl over a pan of simmering water.

Cut the rest of the butter into small cubes, mix with the flour and baking powder in a food processor and blend to crumbs. Add the sugar, lemon rind, eggs, white chocolate and bananas. Whiz until well combined.

Grease a 1.8 litre (3 pint) ring tin. Line the base and sides with nonstick baking paper. Spoon one-quarter of the cake mixture into the base, then drizzle over one-third of the plain dark chocolate. Continue layering the cake mixture and chocolate, finishing with more cake mixture.

Bake in a preheated oven, 180°C (350°F), Gas Mark 4, for 50–60 minutes until the cake feels firm when lightly pressed. Leave in the tin for 10 minutes, then loosen the edges with a knife and turn out on to a wire rack to cool.

Melt the white chocolate in a pan over a bowl of simmering water. Drizzle over the top of the cake. Decorate with the white chocolate chips.

INDEX

PUBLISHER'S NOTE

Standard level spoon measurements are used in all recipes.
1 tablespoon = one 15 ml spoon
1 teaspoon = one 5 ml spoon

Both imperial and metric measurements have been given in all recipes. Use one set of measurements only and not a mixture of both.

This book includes dishes made with nuts and nut derivatives. It is advisable for customers with known allergic reactions to nuts and nut derivatives, and those who may be potentially vulnerable to these allergies, such as babies and children with a family history of allergies, to avoid dishes made with nuts and nut oils. It is also prudent to check the labels of pre-prepared ingredients for the possible inclusion of nut derivatives.

Eggs should be medium unless otherwise stated. The Department of Health advises that eggs should not be consumed raw. This book contains dishes made with raw or lightly cooked eggs. It is prudent for more vulnerable people, such as pregnant and nursing mothers, the elderly, babies and young children, to avoid uncooked or lightly cooked dishes made with eggs. Once prepared, these dishes should be kept refrigerated and eaten promptly.

Milk should be whole (full fat) unless otherwise stated.

Ovens should be preheated to the specific temperature – if using a fan-assisted oven, follow manufacturer's instructions for adjusting the time and the temperature.

All microwave information is based on a 650-watt oven. Follow manufacturer's instructions for an oven with a different wattage.